(Women in Parentheses)

(Women in Parentheses)

Poems by

Catherine Arra

Kelsay Books

Cover design by Shay Culligan
Cover artwork by Nancy Ostrovsky

ISBN: 978-1-950462-11-7

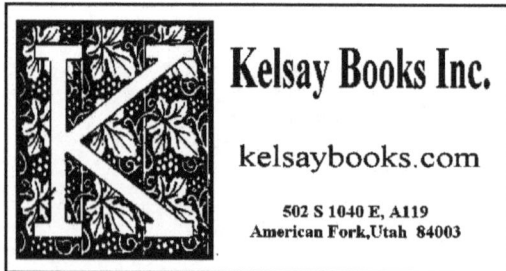

Kelsay Books Inc.

kelsaybooks.com

502 S 1040 E, A119
American Fork, Utah 84003

For Marilyn

Gratitude

To my publisher, Karen Kelsay, of Aldrich Press/Kelsay Books and everyone at the press who worked to make the process of book-making a pleasure.

To Cindy Hochman of "100 Proof" Copyediting Services for her coaching and impeccable proofreading.

To Nancy Ostrovsky for use of her stunning artwork, *Triptych*.

To Jenifer DeBellis, Anne Elezabeth Pluto, and Tim Suermondt for their kind words.

To the Stone Ridge Library Writers for their critical feedback, honesty, and support.

Loving gratitude to my family and friends, and to the man at the center of my life and heart, David Michael Cook.

Other Books by Catherine Arra

Writing in the Ether (2018)

Tales of Intrigue & Plumage (2017)

Loving from the Backbone (2015)

Slamming & Splitting (2014)

Contents

4

5

6

1

Women in Parentheses

Between moon-sliver scythes,
a space to make one's own.

An afterthought, aside,
never subject or verb
(the mighty base sustaining
by the way, *did I mention*).

An interlude, interval, looping
thought, language, worlds seen or not.

Realm of the priestess, goddess,
the swamp-belly bitch bearing the species,

she weaves herself into words, tilts hat to sun
and steps on out.

Weed

I'm common
> as dandelions perpetrating backyard green.
> I connect yellow for images
> lost in growing, stories mowed down by time.
> I play as I did a girl, to become Cinderella,
> a head,
> gown, slippers …
> finding flesh over bones instead.

I'm common
> as dirt, that gritty, dank loam
> caked on worn-down shoes,
> far from scholarly or clever.
> No sestina struts, vexing villanelles,
> no politics or gender,
> no edge, ledge, or experiment.

I'm common
> as earthworms
> late-spring breezes
> flyaway seeds.

My Soul's a Secret Dancer, He Said.

Music is mine.

A fugue, canon
overture, sonata
a four-note rhyme
Mary had a little
gospel blues
jazz hallelujah.

Spirit fire
propulsive desire
heats eight-note octaves
into metered measures
the way an alchemist's
flame transforms.

Magic is what begins
and no music's heard by chance
shh-listen-*shh*
melody
foot-rooted still
carnal-pulse rhythms
beat soul music is
precise, sublime
composing always
composed in its own time.

So come
out into yourself with me
we'll fox-trot rhumba
hop-scotch skip

swivel-sway conga
rock 'n' roll rivet
two-tango waltz
wonder the Milky Way
and maybe
paint the town.

Unsexed

She dreamed
of stallions castrated, of a gnarled forest
in the outback of France, of men prostrate
in hospital beds, naked, their genitals pinched
and spitting semen, of drowning in the glass statue doll
she was with him, lips painted red, the rest transparent.

If she moved, she'd shatter. If she didn't, she'd fill
with water invisible as her skin. She didn't move, for fear
of bloodied geldings, and gurgled to Ophelia's death.

She is the ornament on his bed table,
a waterscape instead of snow.
Pick her up, peer through her. See the red folds
swirling in the vestibule of her sex; soft, undulating,
penetrable more than he, fearing his coming
as if she had been a thief.

In the Name of

Mother's abandonment
wringing hands, pacing penny-counting poverty.
Father's entitlement
new wife, family, seaside vacations.
Choked-girl rage and slight—a concoction like acid
chafes skin, its scent Daddy's sabotage with a sheen,
slick like ice.

Nothing, absolutely nothing, would ever stick to her again.

Eyes cast downward
honeyed docility is masterful
elevates a whine to whimsy, clutches
hanky in palm
dots   nose   lips   chest
in the name of   the father   the father   the father

evokes exquisite pity, exhales airy alms.

The diminutive serves her
stitches a cape of embroidered flora—
decades of blighted blooms to drape shoulders
wrap tight.

Nothing, absolutely nothing, will ever be taken from her again.

Espionage

Nineteen—watching an espionage flick
main spy says to rival spy,
When you know a lie is a lie, you begin to learn the truth.

Twenty-nine—the good wife until
hubby-hunk is cheating. She asks, *Is it so?*
He says, *No, no, no.*

Thirty-three—divorced, edging recovery
collides with the letter Mother signed, *love*
to Father's best friend. She asks, *Is it so?*

Mother says, *Yes and no.* She'll quit,
do the right thing. A month later Father puddles at her feet.
It wasn't a fling.

Thirty-five—feeling orphaned and feral
likes sap in trees, honey in her tease
is temptress to a virgin-hood of older men.

Brings one home, unbuttons his hard-on
in her big brassy bed. He asks, *Do you love me?*
She says, *Yes, yes, yes.*

Thirty-nine—a spy in her house of tricks
cataloging fictions, footnoting crimes
indexing brevity of truth on overwritten pages.

When you know a lie is a lie, you begin to learn the truth.

2

Tchotchkes

They live in shadow boxes, each perched as a rare bird
in her domain to be admired from afar,
never approached or touched.

Exclusive personas cultivated in crooked girlhoods,
curated over years—the souvenir princess, the freak,
the erudite scholar, the honey pot ...

They could be thimbles all—intricately painted
in porcelain flourish, calculated allure,
hollow caverns yawning underneath,

never to be your friends.

A Gender Thing

Weekdays he knows he should feel guilty
about being unemployed. He watches her labor out of bed,
wrestle with a wardrobe, and lumber down stairs.

"Getting up now," he says on a rain-soaked 6:00 a.m.
when no one sane or guiltless abandons a warm bed.

Weekends he offers flowers, cleans house. A man and a woman.
She blushes gratitude, cooks up a fancy dinner, lights two
candles, lies soft on sheets, missionary position (of course).

Monday she labors out of bed, wrestles with a wardrobe,
lumbers down stairs, and admonishes sleep.
A job she can no longer endure.

Three Women on a Rack

I have a friend who tells me
she's having an affair. She's bold and brash
cuts me off in mid-sentence, wears war paint for blush
holds a sword at the door of her womb.

I have another friend who is having two affairs
one on the East Coast, the other out West. Her lovers
are married with kids. She's a double-holstered hunter.
Makes it safer and the bull's-eye clear.

They sit at my kitchen table, smoking cigarettes
drinking scotch. What to do? I shrug,
try not to judge. I mean, who am I
but a middle-aged divorcée, a survivor in exile?

Sure, I live alone, unwed, having unhooked
my G-string from the horns of a dilemma,
donated my trousseau to the rummage sale at the Catholic church.
Crawled on all fours out of the desert
of dinners at six, laundry on Saturdays, Red Dot specials
and sex on weekends, whether I wanted it or not.
The ultimate blow, though, the crater of disaster
was "the other woman" like my friends' "other men."
Oh hey, everybody's a thief one time or another.

So I listen to her and her laments
and wonder if monogamy might stand a better chance in hell.
They're sick a lot, my friends. Colds, flu,
sniffles and coughs clogging up passageways with phlegm.

It's gluey, the guilt of self-betrayal,
buying silk boxers out of the joint checking account,
punishing old hubby-cakes for being a cowboy
when he should be a poet, or a poet
when he should be a cowboy.

Clint Eastwood in Romeo's tights, racing Lancelot's horse
along the edge of a fault line. He's the guy they want.
Pour him out. Drink him up like a potion,
the transcending orgasm. Fly me to the moon
or anywhere out of mediocrity and another damn video
with a happy ending.

I don't want to be like my friends,
a wet pussy drying up and parched,
thinking the milk-blood of men is the balm that heals.
I'm scared and lonely, watching the woods for clues.

I want to live deep in the forest,
fertile and green. In the center of a swamp
with alligators and mud. In the wild,
where life abides by other laws layered deep in the earth,
spinning high above the cerebral cortex of impossible expectations.

I want to live in a jungle untamed, where
life doesn't think about itself, but is,
where my body makes the oils that anoint me
and welcomes my mate, with his guns and his rhymes,
home.

A Hobo's Hunger

She calls at midnight,
her bewitching hour when Jack Daniels bottoms up
and she bottoms out. Her lifeblood
spirals down the cross of her femininity,
slithers between forty-something thighs,
glues her into a mountain of refuse
too immense to burn, bulldoze, or
bury at sea.

In desperation she rockets it
along the vector-path of phone lines. Crash lands
in beds of her Once Upon a Time Princes
who toted golden slippers. The hobos
along love's way who stumbled into her alley,
rifled through her legs looking to make
a meal out of a discarded hard roll.
Finding it buried beneath coffee grinds,
microwave dinners for one. Devouring it
because she let them, all for a shot at the slippers.

No matter she smelled of booze and cigarettes,
her skin etched and coarse
from the strain of growing old.
The creamy pink flesh hiding between bones
like the still-moist center of yesterday's brioche
was refuge enough for the iron rod of rejection.
The dark alley between starvation
and the Once Upon a Time Queen of Banquets.

Susan, Oh Susan

(On July 22, 1995, Susan Smith was convicted of the drowning death of her two sons, three-year-old Michael and 14-month-old Alexander.)

Was it loneliness? The kind that yawns
and swallows rage, the one thing left?
The kind that wakes at 3 a.m. and empties the bed?
Did you think you'd never be kissed or sexed or noticed again?
Did you beg and barter the night for help, for the sweet massage
and breaking ground of his hard cock, any cock to separate
flesh before you suffocated? Did you need it and hate it
and need it anyway, his foul breath and semen, before you erased
entirely? And did you say you'd do anything, even blame a black man,
anything, to be ruptured past solitude and the hum of a woman alone?
Is that what drove you to the lake?
Did you deliver your babies to the womb you lost to loneliness?

Speak 1

Without a voice, I mean *your* voice, girl,
backed by your backbone,

not the *crapola* lies you've swallowed
since you could listen, talk, imitate,

not the things Mommy said *good girls don't do,*

not the 4-H Willing Worker you were sewing aprons,
cup-caking your way to homemaker blue-ribbon fame,

not practicing ancient versions of yourself
properly fearful of:

she's the slut type, nasty, demanding,
doesn't-know-her-place type

until you become the whining con,
cunningly powerless, pussy-footing gossip,
sneaky, silenced type
forever sabotaging, dirt-talking, eye-rolling
women who dare, and do, speak.

Speak 2

for Linda

She reminds me who I was, finds me
in the tumult of divorce from the man
I thought I knew, not as well as I know her, the girl
who once sidled up to me—high school teenagers
at a library table and said,

> "What are you reading?"

> "Existentialism."

> "Tell me everything you know about that."

Brash girl, stranger
sat down uninvited, challenged what I knew,
asked me to say it.
How dare she pull me out, expect me to, but I did,

and now he's leaving after 20 years.
Legalese served as tepid as last night's meal,
not saying, telling, why, how, or who.

Singed by his iciness I never thought for me,
his indifference to grief clamoring up and down stairs
to tether an unbridled will to leave.

Raw, unrivaled, the paralyzing sting
of abandonment avalanches, until she calls
from 1,500 miles away and says,

> "Tell me everything you know about that."

Pundit

There will come a time
when everything ridiculed, broken down
rallied tender sensibilities to tears
everything hated, hauled to soapbox
grandstanding, scoffed down academic nose
scratched glasses, unzipped fly
everything mocked because it mocked
the face you wanted
not the face you had
everything deconstructed for the ridiculous joy
of being nothing special, including the way
she loved you anyway
will drop you to knees
invisible man
begging, blathering
licking life for one last
taste of frivolity.

3

Child

I conceived you
in the rush of cicadas
rising from roots
in silver ribbons of salmon
running from sea to stream.

By the clock that grinds and chimes
the hours of mating
by instinct
greater than personal will
my days of drifting ended
my communing in oceans stopped.

Driven upward to unholy light
to sparring in foreign climates,
I dodged concrete
eluded nets and *Evinrudes*.

Despite myself I came
to sing and spawn
to open this womb to seed
and die.

That Untended

sleeps in cool spaces
stirs and pulls sheets, exposes a nakedness
when we were lovers.

Time imposes separation, forgets.
But the past, comfortable in interstices,
dreams with ease, spins in the soft blur of the ceiling fan.
I roll into your neck, taste again satin skin
find our scent and edge closer
until a cluster of child's toys scratches my thighs:
a plastic hammer, sandbox shovels, a doll.

On the flight
mother and child opposite me, the daughter
a new butterfly unfurling in her mother's lap
fingers forming words, reaching to plant them
in mother's full lips
the two of them unfurling in their rapture.
I couldn't look away, stop the want.
Told you, breathless
barely through the gate: *A child?*
After the project, you said. *When it's finished.*
Never was.

Video

A
lop-sided
scotch pine
garland loops
wedding band
gold glistening
'round
ghost fingers
hooking
stained glass
and
candy canes
placing
tinsel tiers
in
evergreen
for
the Angel
atop
Christmas
our last.

Quick Read

He is the space in her spiral of activity
the guttural pause when she speaks
omitting a word or two, a name
changing the tense from present to past.
It's a purposeful task—
editing memory to hard copy.

Fall Back

Must not be anything worth saving
after Daylight Saving Time.

The garden's dead, clocks surrender to night
but I think I remember the past ten years—

the first dahlias eaten by ground moles,
getting up, going to work, coming home,

a turkey, a tree, the same circle of heads
around a table.

I know Mother died one of those years,
disrupting the counting of plates. Was January, I think.

She walked out into the snow, lay down, and
then the wash, the ironing, the wash,

the ironing, dahlia roots chewed, cat hair on stairs,
getting up, going to work, coming home.

I think I fell in love once after the divorce
maybe he didn't—

then the time changed, surrendered to night,
a turkey, a tree, the same circle of heads.

I seem to recall taking up aerobics, giving up meat,
cigarettes, changing jobs,

getting up, going to work, coming home.
This year I gave up dahlias and planted marigolds

but the time changed and the garden died anyway.
Ten years from now I'll remember

loving you after the clocks changed
and there wasn't enough time.

Maybe:

November rain on early nightfall
soon after parting made the long-distance wait
too soon to look back
flash-freezing time, erasing passage from him to you.

Muddled memory, mistakes in idle time
hurled heartbreak knowing no difference
between alone is a feeling
alone never forgets.

I want too, worry too, wish too
much or not at all know why
I called you "liar."

Somewhere in dredged-earth mud
rainstorms lost you to remembrance—
a bride's blind faith, coin-flipped joy,
and the lie he told.

We enjoy our apologies for the crossings they mark.

Mid-winter Blues

The air inside is old and sleepy.
The air outside is old and biting. Both hurt
and there's nowhere to go.

She catalog-shops for late spring and summer,
glossy pages of delicious sand and light.
She tastes the sea, feels her warm, creamy skin kissed
in the flowing silk dress. She's leaning against the palm,
hair thick with ocean salt; arms, legs, and hidden belly bronzed.
She's fully a woman now. No sniffles, sneezes, low-back stress.
No raw red blotches flanking eyes and mouth.

She calls the toll-free number. Chats with Denise,
sweet Denise has that dress in seven colors.
She orders olive, for the muted green of morning breezes,
for bird songs, and reflections on the lake.

In three days the dress will be hers. She'll slip it on,
peek through the embroidery and slits,
pale-skinned and pasty with nowhere to go.

Don't Read His Poetry Before Bed

for Matthew Dickman

About suicide, brothers, all the ways a broken heart makes you crazy. Like Mom said, *Don't eat that before you go to sleep; it'll give you nightmares.* Ice cream, cake heavy and sweet, not the black tar licorice of his poetry turning, twisting the way she warned; a charley horse in the hamstring strangles you up to pee, to break the reruns like menopausal laps of sweat and chills; that's what his poetry does to you; it bleeds you out until you're old, and innocence playing catch in the backyard cripples down that leg, pools in bed with you at 2:08 a.m.; his damn misery not in the least your own, drives you up again to drink glasses of cold water to dilute his anguish the way you water down too much booze, making you nauseated, so now it's your biology keeping you awake, not him.

Like the Big Bang

I slide through years
since we parted
not comprehending
the span of time I'm slicing
with tomatoes for the *caprese* salad
I will place before you, and it will be
summer and savory, the zing of basil
snipped from the terracotta pot on the patio
just outside the door where some things are forever—
it's true
that happens between people
living and dead, the psyche slices back
the story because
time
in cradled cocoons
in silk-spun secrets and promises
goes on like that
expanding and
never out of reach.

4

White Spaces

After black, before red,
and the bold mixing of Picasso colors
are white spaces. In the skylight portal
above her bed where the moon courts Venus,
defies Orion's sword. In the perfect spill
of November dawn while she breathes through a flute
to find December. In the time between the night before
the morning after, the shower and the towel.
In the unmarked calendar with forgotten dates.
In the room at the end of the hall where
one made business deals, another wrote poetry
she never entered. On the wall in the room
at the end of the hall, in the house she's lived
with transients, today she hung a nude
painted black and red.

Dead Letters

I can no longer read
emails to *Lara,* my screen name
before the split-up
before I added the number *62*
to disassociate him—me
in time, habitat, and cyberspace.

But *Lara* still lives
receives pieces of me gone afield
stores in my personal Iron Mountain
rants, rebuttals, love notes
sent by accidental numeric omission.

I imagine *Lara* spying
on my life
wonder if she misses me, remotely likes me.
I sometimes write to her on purpose
sweet-toned words
like a bereaved spouse.

Nothing.

I try hacking with old passwords
a few other tricks.
I need to reach her, hear her voice
the silly way she makes verbs out of nouns
like *passengering, breakfasting*
teases in closings, seduces with spaces.

Nothing.

Could there be
a dead letters email office
where a ghost of myself
fades with old photographs,
perfume, and ink?

I'll keep writing to you, *Lara,*
without the *62*
keep trying to make contact.

Giro del Cassero, 16

On steep *Via Raffaello*
perpetual brick sealed in Renaissance sweat
climbs and opens to an occasional archway, or *giro*—
a tunneled turn, alley cat refuge circling around back
to a blooming courtyard, morning laundry dripping
into terracotta pots, or a vista beyond city walls
before it returns to the street.

Primo piano, on the first floor, really the second floor
is my *piccolo appartamento* with a single window leveled high
above the street that pools in the piazza below.
Sun-worn shutters, cracked marble green on weathered wood
serve as screen, shade, and silence.
My window-box geranium on the massive stone ledge
is pink and thirsty.
I offer bottled water before hauling in the last valise.
Urbino, Italia.

Ma senza di te. Without you.
Exiled in spring as Easter lilies closed and Tuscan sun
dried palms too brittle to curl into crucifixes.
I've crossed and re-crossed the ocean
in fits, sleep, tears, in planes
lost the longitude, latitude, the tiny mapped square
the time zone, vest-pocket letter
the heartbeats and breaths that mark
the geography and boundaries of love.

Vado e torno a me stesso, al piccolo appartamento
con i fiori nella finestra ed un letto singolo.
Sono giunta cosi, al Giro del Cassero
che comincia e finisce sulla Via Raffaello.

52

I go, and return to myself, to the small apartment
with flowers in the window and a single bed.
I have come like this to *Giro del Cassero*
that begins and ends on *Via Raffaello.*

Things That Work

She says she's interested in how
things work, not how they don't:
a marriage, pinning each other to the
very word with a vow and a list;
a budding friendship nipped in one-
sided want.

How things don't work, we all know
tell the therapist, lawyer, family
friends, ourselves. Tell it clear
round up a well-armed posse.

She did, she didn't, he did, he didn't
he said, she said
you, you, you
said, didn't, did.

Things that work don't ask, insist
stomp off kickin' up dust
threaten, blame.

The way hydrogen bonds
to oxygen, gravity balances opposites
a spark catches, a seed germinates
the tiniest atom alights
a gift given
to have without owning, without
taking what is not to be taken.

She says
How do you know he won't meet
someone new, want to marry?
How do you know?
She clenches fists, wrings hands as if
to squeeze the answer drop by drop
from humid air.

After the Flood

for Beverly

She's full of a sorrow she can't name, a levee under stress
backing the might of a bloated river. If a word is uttered
accidentally, a name mentioned, a gun fires through trigger fingers.
Her rain god answers and she cracks like Humpty Dumpty.
Tears mark the fault lines, map trails that have led her astray.
I wrap my arms around her need, embrace my own.
We turn to face the late-afternoon sea
ebbing now, before the tide reverses. I say, cry.
Cry until you see land again, lay bare feet on new ground.
Cry for Daddy, dead by the time you were twelve,
for Granny, turned into a pillar of cancer,
for the solidarity of childhood lost in middle age,
for the lies of romance, especially romance.
Cry until the waters break you with every dam and levee
and you have drenched the soil of a womanhood unturned.
Cry yourself to your knees. Wail for women everywhere.
Cry until you are again an art form, the original mold. Then
celebrate all that has eaten you down to raw bones.

After Divorce

A new narrative
without labels, husband—wife.

A flooded washout
no ownership
claims, entitlements
polarized showdowns
walk twelve paces, turn-draw-shoot.

Muddy waters settle.
Capes, masks, and superheroes
return to Marvel Land.
Barbie and Ken
to the cardboard box.
Mommy and Daddy
to their beds
out of ours.

We're walking
a trestle bridge
above the old canal town
where water and tracks cross.

Root Canal

Fire furrows up nostrils
clear through the third eye
blinds black a history
she doesn't recognize
erases white every lie
spoken or suggested.

Lightning sears
down & up
the collapsing corridor
of her spine
turning red to orange
to yellow to green
a spinning elliptical
until a blue explosion
unboundaries

and
she emerges
like an amethyst
out of shattered dirt.

5

Old School Tie

November drizzle. A narrow sidewalk.
Our double picket lines
train in opposite directions. I wonder,
am I moving forward or backward?

We loop at distant ends—rubber bands,
revolving in flattened orbits.
The sign I carry
is a war cry. I'm silent.

A man says, "My first picket was in '78."
A woman answers, "My job is gone."
The School Board extends no Hallmark regrets,
no pink-slip sympathy—a motion and a vote.

Earth spins dusk to night.
Union President chants,
"What do we want?"
"A contract."
"When do we want it?"
"Now."
"What?"
"A contract."
"When?"
"Now."
"What?"
"A contract. A contract. Now."

I like the fever of naughty justice
though my feet are cold.
I want to believe we'll make a difference
but suspect this line has no end.

Mother Teacher

I greet you, alphabetize
steer your course.

I assign, assess
punctuate, correct.
I disengage tangled thought.

Priestess of parallel structure
mistress of mental fortitude,
logic, and grace,
I bleed my decrees
into the margins of your frailty.

I dictate, disseminate,
direct, and discipline
while I wait
the weeks, semester,
sometimes the year
for the seed of who you are
waiting in the silver of your eyes.

Transparent Pants

We are a small family, ten or twelve counting me.
Seventh-grade Basic English, recently
renamed from the pejorative "Special Curriculum,"
or "Spe-Cu" for short.

Downtown kids—each with a story.
I'm teaching a lesson in subject-verb agreement,
still convinced presentation is everything.

They've been willing, but now halfway through
Donte raises his hand and blurts,
"Yo, Teacher."

I stop. Turn, holding my chalk.

With great urgency he says, "Roger has a boner. Look."
He points. "Show her, Rog."

Roger springs from his seat, stands with puffed chest.
I look down at his too-tight, transparent, summer-white pants,
yellow and gray from too many or too few washings.

There it is—his swollen stalk etched perfectly,
and larger than I would have imagined for his thirteen years.

Roger beams.

We all look.
We are awed by this brief hiatus in higher learning.

Now, there are choices a teacher can make
and I think of them all.
Finally I say, "That's very nice, Roger.
Thank you for showing us."

Roger, as pleased as a student
who just received an *A,* smiles shyly
and sits down.

We go back to subjects and verbs.
Presentation is everything.

Coming Back

I don't want to go. Why should I? I want to go outside. For a ride. All the windows open. Fresh clean spring air. Sun on the windshield. On my face. Warm. Bright. Put on my shades. Turn on the tunes. Ride. Yeah, ride and glide with the afternoon tide. I don't want to go. Why should I?

Ms. Finn rose from behind the chrome and Formica desk in room 408. Her next class would begin in ten minutes, English 9 in room 307. She left the plan book, the red pen, the canvas bag bloated with vocabulary and compositions. She walked out of the classroom, down the corridor, through the main entrance, and into April.

No oscillating fluorescent lights. No buzzers or bells. No ricocheted ruckuses reverberating off concrete walls. No nothing. Just a day. A Thursday. Any day.

Ms. Finn walked to her car. She rolled down the windows, started and revved the engine, put her in drive, and headed south.

At 12:40 the seventh-period bell blasted. Like rats unleashed in an experimental box, bodies swarmed and scurried. At 12:43 twenty-two ninth-graders romped into 307. At 12:44 they had almost landed in their seats. At 12:50 Mr. Worth in room 308 could no longer bear the noise.

"Where's Ms. Finn? Sit down. Get away from that window. Ms. Finn? Is she here?"
"No, man, she ain't here."
"Does this mean we get a free period?"
"Sit down and be quiet."

Mr. Worth phoned the main office. Mr. Strong, the principal, arrived in a flash. At 1:00 an announcement cut through, contaminating the precious calm of ninety-four budding lessons. "Ms. Finn. Will Ms. Finn call the main office? Immediately, Ms. Finn."

But Ms. Finn was out of earshot. She was sunbathing on the warm rocky banks of the Hudson River.

"Please see Mr. Strong as soon as possible," read the note placed in Ms. Finn's mailbox the next morning. Ms. Finn obeyed responsibly. She was third in a line of delinquents seated just outside the principal's office. Each held a Discipline Referral; Ms. Finn, her note.

"Whatcha doin' here, Ms. Finn? Ain't cha got a class now?"
"Mr. Strong has asked to see me."
"You in trouble, Ms. Finn?"
The secretary's eyes bulleted threats against any notion of answering honestly.
"No. Mr. Strong just wants to see me. Do you mind me sitting with you?"
"No, man, no. Wanna go first? You can have my chair."

The double hardwood doors of Mr. Strong's office opened. The awesome air of authority filled the waiting room. A peevish-looking black-leather-jacketed truant shuffled out, defused of defiance.

"Ms. Finn, if you please," gestured the principal.
Ms. Finn rose and crossed through the doors.

"Hang loose, Ms. Finn."

"Yeah, man, stay cool."

"Be quiet. You're next," warned the secretary. The double doors closed. The latch clicked.

"How are you today, Ms. Finn?"

"I'm fine. Thank you."

"Was there an emergency yesterday afternoon? Something that required your immediate attention?"

"No, sir. There was no emergency."

"I see, then. You were ill?"

"No, sir."

The principal shifted in his chair, placed his elbows on the desk, hands firmly clasped.

"Ms. Finn, what was the pressing situation that caused you to leave this building in the middle of the school day, thereby deserting both your seventh- and eighth-period classes without any warning or notice?"

"There was no pressing situation, Mr. Strong. I cut."

"You what?"

"I cut."

Mr. Strong swiveled his chair sideways and stood.

"Ms. Finn, you have taught here for thirteen years. You have an outstanding record and reputation. This is not the type of behavior I expect from you or any professional. What is the problem?"

"No problem, sir. I simply had to do it."

"What ever for?"

"To come back."

Dismissed, Ms. Finn walked the long glass hallway to her classroom. The yellow wash of sunlight drenched and warmed her. She entered her twelfth-grade literature class, already seated and waiting, monitored by the assistant vice principal.

"Yesterday we talked about individual responsibility and freedom in relation to Camus's *The Stranger.* Last night you wrote a journal response. Let's hear your thoughts.

A dozen or so hands rose in offerings.

Retirement

Third day of rain or almost rain
side-stepping storms
slight tightness in back neck
rising to headache
and I've hardly noticed
the date, August 24th.
All the waning
summers before another school year
from kindergarten to turning
in the chalk, the dread of losing time.
All those years in front,
and now
another September
sneaking up
foot-printing the wet,
gray-laced lawn, backyard-stalking
a new dread, not of losing summer
but what to do
with unfettered time, lest it shimmer,
the last raindrop
on the Rose of Sharon,
and wink away.

Justice: A Letter of Resignation

My scales are tarnished and rusty, my robes faded and threadbare. I'm nothing more than a sooty statue, a museum piece, a testament to abandoned ideals. My body is skeletal, my bones fragile with your cancerous fear. Like my sisters, Athena and Liberty, I'm shamed by your neglect, your complicity and cowardice, raped by your greed, stupidity, your ridiculous illusions of power. You dressed us up like Barbie dolls with fancy gold scales, torches, and olive branches. You gave us the job of symbol and archetype. You even made us female. Then you laid your humanity on us the way you have crippled God with your salvation. We quit. Not because we want to, but because you silenced us. Said hit the showers, keep the props. Said we want the other guy, the predator with tattoos and chains, the one in black leather who spikes his hair and paints it red. We want him. He's sexy. You're not.

6

(   )

Old cat on the porch
howls and is still.
She settles into floorboards pooled in sun
and practices dying.

Bones inevitably press down
into the dirty gravity
of living close to death
but not the old woman.

Her flaccid arms flail
in another soapbox surge
of chronic caterwauling,
carping, and complaint.

Her endless ballad
of simpering, whining,
of midnight barking
from a bottomless, waterless well
keep her forever awake

and her body grows ever more fearful
of the
(   )
raging in the basement.

Evidence

I.

Each day, no rain
the lake recedes, sand emerges
littered with dirt, sea stones
shell spirals, a lost feather.
Once, this whole area was covered in saltwater,
says my neighbor. His three grandchildren
troll the edge in excavating leaps and glee.
I smell an old sea
the rotted death of centuries
taste a salty fertility on skin.
A jute rope, buried in thirds,
loops to land and out into
aquatic wreaths; eel grass
sways in a world silent to me.
I imagine sounds turtles make
propelling titanic armor, the hum-glide to the top
ringing a shattered surface
inflections of fish gills
in unmetered staccato, sucking, pumping
the triangle cinch
of the sand crane's toes.
And then, the groaning bottom
belches up its dead.
On the walkway squealing kids
display mutilated mollusks
partial turtle shells, pinchers, bird bones
alligator teeth.

II.

She was rolled back
with the Persian carpet
purchased in Turkey on honeymoon
62 years ago.
In the underlayers
the collected dust of living:
jewels, cankers, choices made or not
outcomes expected or not
ghosts celebrating long past midnight.
When he passed
and was rolled out
she called a charity to take clothing
boxed his history in customized memoirs
for each kid—stories they wanted to hear.
She sold antiques, art collected abroad,
diamonds, gold.
And when they rolled up the carpet, trucked it away
she watched from glass framing the sea below
her footprints fresh in carpet dust
like sand before the wave.

Stain of an Angel

Sitting by the single window
a crescent moon in black leather, the woman
looks out at the length of winter
and back to the morning coffee
she spilled on the beige carpet
now working itself into a stain.

She's ashamed of that stain
leaching into her dignity, a window
for all to see how old age carpets
down like concrete, cracks skin, leaving a woman
no hope for lipstick, blush, a cosmetic the color of coffee
to stain back time and help her winter

over losses of husband and home. Winter
down this season of verticals that stain
palms and map roads ahead. A nice cup of coffee
in the morning helps. She sips it by the window
in the two-room senior home where the woman
must balance it from hardwood to carpet.

It's there to trip her every time, that carpet
in the middle, a bull's-eye in the beige winter
of incontinence, meal seatings, dementia, and a woman
she hardly recognizes. She turns away but the stain
betrays her, mocks her in the paned window
reflecting back the pooling darkness of cold coffee.

She remembers Papa, gone now, bringing his coffee
a freshly brewed demitasse, a biscotti, the salon carpet
rich wool, the Christmas tree in the center window
of holidays filled with children, grandchildren, winter
wonder, crystal glassware, and wine to stain
linens she embroidered as a young woman.

Papa comes to her now and she is again that woman.
Each night, he says, *Come with me,* and brings to her coffee.
He extends his hand, guides her past the stain
at the foot of the bed, treading softly over the carpet
to the door, down the hallway and into winter.
They pause a moment and look back through the window.

When he leaves, the woman lies below the window.
Her arms fan to sculpt the stain of an angel in a carpet
of snow that melts like hot coffee, pooling in the center of winter.

The Particular Preference of Ghosts

Estate sale. Daughter, sixty-something, hip-hefty, bossy
sits living room center with cash box. Red hair splays
unruly spikes, cinched by a straw visor. Her voice
booms and circles corridors.

Neighbors swoop in, grab, bargain, leave.
Open-mouth dumpster awaits the rest.

Mother passed last month
was meaning to yard-sale, weed through.
Oh, such accumulations. What to keep?
Let go? What would George have done?

She glides now between
the walnut credenza and dining table
fingertips a particular crystal champagne flute:
the delicate frilled edge, the purple stem like a lily.
She raises it to toast all the things necessary,
then drifts to the violet sofa, darkened in twilight, tagged
$100.00 or best offer, and is gone.

I nestle the fluted glass in my bag.
$5.00 for the only one left of two.

God's Waiting Room

When I retire and move to Florida
I'm going to float on two neon pool tubes, visor in place,
towel securely clipped to lounge.

I'll say,

*Hey, whatta 'bout those poor slobs up there in New York
& Jersey buried up to their asses, 4 degrees—
Geez almighty, do we have the life or what?*

I'm going to set the weather app
to Chicago, Detroit, Buffalo. Ha!

I'm going to sniff out early bird specials
and say,

*Whatta meal, I have to tell ya. That cup of soup, I mean,
more like a bowl
or you can get a nice salad, always fresh an'
a choice of entrée with three sides, not the usual two,
dessert, coffee ...
oh, an' yeah, a drink, yeah, a real bar drink
an' all for 9.99.
You believe it? Was outta this world, let me tell ya,
an' I'm tellin' ya, that steak, it just melted in my mouth
an' the wife
she had the tilapia—nice an' fresh, she said, grilled just so
not all dried out.*

When I retire and move to Florida
I'm going to have it my way.

Whatta life, I'm tellin' ya.
Worked 40 stinkin' years for this.

Nah, an' I ain't gonna notice your little baby lizard
sunnin' on the terrace
an' I didn't feel bad when I took off the end of its tail—
I mean, what the hell—it was an accident.

An' I don't give a frig about that bird noise,
oh excuse me ... songs.
Just close the damn door.
Whatta ya always talkin' at me about the sun risin' an' fallin'
makin' the edges of livin' an dyin'?

For Chrissake, go write a poem or somethin'.
Me, I'll just wait here for the old Reaper, enjoyin' myself,
an' when the bastard shows up, I ain't gonna give him
the right time of day neither.

Water Aerobics

Four women stomping
down pool laps
cajole the Bistro owner to pipe
out the music—LOUD.
I forget the book.

Big woman
with the biggest voice starts it.
Her entourage in varying degrees
of size and volume pipe in,
telling tales
about that first lay; drunken legs straddling
young buttocks
in back seats, closets, cornfields.

Sixy-somethings
loving themselves young.

Then in unison, no cues
the white visor, straw hat
black cap, and pink turban
pick up step with the beat,
punch air, singing *Rockin' Robin.*

We're all rockin', bare toes keeping time.
Man next to me shakes his head
gives up on *The Sunday Times,* leaves
as they jump, midriffs bulging, and
shout *Tequila!*

Someone on the ladder shouts back
"No, margarita!"

It's that mix—that zeitgeist

between 1955 and '75
the Cold War and Vietnam

when
What it is ain't exactly clear

When we
fought the law ...

needed
Help, a *Dream Lover,* a *Dream*
It was
The Time of the Season
to *Give Peace ...*

Take a load off ...

Singin'
... sha la,
la la dee dah

Do you remember
when we used to ...

Just like that.

Christmas Eve / Sex After Sixty

A man, a woman
on a couch. He's in a terry robe;
she, a kimono.
Side by side, they fit.
Her cat rests on his chest, purring.
Tree lights multiply in French doors.
Clothes litter hardwood,
dangle from rocker arms.
Teetering on a candlestick
is something of hers,
white and lacy,
swaying between
movie frames, where for now
they need no criticism
or applause.
She laughs at their irreverence.
He meets pleasure
grinning on her lips.
The cat thumps to the floor,
robes slide away.

With You

for David

I.

Twilight settles the day's debts.
Sun, long on the horizon, sinks to ease
morning transgressions, afternoon slips of tongue,
casts a forgiving glow upon the table
set with good wine, savory olives, and cheese.
On the lake, water birds peck, pluck, dive
to harvest one last meal before nightfall.
White egrets like tiki lights flicker on the island
dense with green, roost to coo the colony to sleep.
You reach across 115,000 heartbeats, 24,000 breaths,
lift my fingers in your palm,
"Have I told you today *I love you?*"

II.

Where is that peaceful place—
the seaside, a mountaintop, the woods?
Breathe … relax. Let muscles soften.
Take the tongue from the roof of the mouth.
Loosen the jaw. Let go now, and breathe.

I'm in the billowing cloud of our bed,
leg draped over your thigh, nose nested
in the fur of your chest, cheek rising and falling
with the tides of your breathing, your scent.
Our middle-aged biology a communal chorus of waking.

III.

If this
heat, skin, breath, and our scent
and this
backbone, breast, buttocks
could arc and bend time infinitely,
and this
could be death, I'd be okay with that.

Acknowledgments

Grateful acknowledgment is made to the editors of the following publications in which these poems first appeared, sometimes in different versions.

Compass: "Stain of an Angel"
Dying Dahlia Review: "Three Women on a Rack"
First Literary Review-East: "Justice: A Letter of Resignation," "Tchotchkes," "Things That Work," "Women in Parentheses"
Flutter Poetry Journal: "Giro del Cassero, 16"
Funny in Five Hundred: "Transparent Pants"
Ginosko Literary Journal: "Dead Letters," "The Particular Preference of Ghosts," "Video"
Gloom Cupboard: "Evidence"
MockingHeart Review: "That Untended"
Nixes Mate Review: "Water Aerobics"
Pink Panther Magazine: "After the Flood," "Child," "Fall Back," "Unsexed"
Panoply, A Literary Zine: "Like the Big Bang"
Scarlet Leaf Review: "God's Waiting Room"
Switched-on Gutenberg: "White Spaces"
The Timberline Review: "Don't Read His Poetry Before Bed"

About the Author

Catherine Arra is a former high school English and writing teacher. Since leaving the classroom in 2012, her poetry and prose have appeared in numerous literary journals online and in print, and in several anthologies. She is the author of *Writing in the Ether* (Dos Madres Press, 2018) and three chapbooks, *Tales of Intrigue & Plumage* (FutureCycle Press, 2017), *Loving from the Backbone* (Flutter Press, 2015), and *Slamming & Splitting* (Red Ochre Press, 2014). Arra is a native of the Hudson Valley in upstate New York, where she lives most of the year, teaches part-time, and facilitates local writing groups. In winters she migrates to the Space Coast of Florida.

Find her at www.catherinearra.com

Kelsay Books

www.ingramcontent.com/pod-product-compliance
Lightning Source LLC
Chambersburg PA
CBHW022202080426
42734CB00006B/553